Researched and Collated by Sharon Halstead

Copyright © 2018 by Sharon Halstead
Petitepeds® is a registered trademark of Sharon Halstead
All rights reserved, including the right to reproduce this book or portions thereof in any form whatsoever. Affiliate links may be used, which is at not cost to you.

Credits
Cover graphics, book illustrations and Graphic Design by Karen Hue
E-book creation by Luca Funari, lucafunari@hotmail.com
Author and images: Luisa Kearney, ©OnlinePersonalStylist.com, Sharon Halstead © PetitePeds

Contact
Email: sales@petitepeds.com.au
Website AU: www.petitepeds.com.au
Website US: www.petitepeds.co

Melbourne, Australia

Cataloguing
National Library of Australia Cataloguing-in Publication Date
Sharon Halstead's Petite Fashion, the Long and Short of It
Fashion

INTRODUCTION The Long and Short of it

Petite Fashion

I HAVE A DREAM... a dream to help Petite ladies!

Welcome

The aim of this book is to provide you with numerous tips (sourced, thoroughly researched and then compiled into one easy to read, direct and explicit beautiful book). I am confident it contains quality content to assist all you beautiful petite ladies out there who struggle with dressing your petite frames and feet.

Now in business for a few years, I have heard all the stories of woe and frustration from my petite customers, not just about shoes but clothing and fashion in general. It has been my catch cry that "Dressing a petite lady is different to dressing an average woman, period."

With a firm interest in being the authority on anything petite, I decided to invest in creating a book to dress the unique petite frame, and combined with a qualified fashion stylist so that we could assist our customers. This book is a culmination of all the research, sourced from qualified stylists, customer feedback and good old-fashioned trial and error, into this very unique E-book targeted at petite ladies. As the saying goes, "necessity is the mother of invention" so it was out of a dire need for change that this e-book was born.

Remember this book is essentially a reference book, not to be digested in one sitting, but rather to be referred to whenever you have a fashion dilemma or want to know what goes with what, what will suit your body shape or face shape or skin colour or what accessory to match for your height etc.

I would love to get any feedback so please feel free to contact me with comments, questions or suggestions at

Yours fashionably

Sharron Halstead
Founder, Petitepeds

Contents

CHAPTER 1	Petite Women – what is petite?...	7
CHAPTER 2	How to dress to suit your age...	9
CHAPTER 3	What is Style and how to achieve it?..	15
CHAPTER 4	What Not to Wear	23
CHAPTER 5	A Look-book of Ideal Clothing...	31
CHAPTER 6	Different Body Shapes..	46
CHAPTER 7	Size Gudie to Petite Sizes...	80
	How to Measure Your Foot	86
BIOGRAPHY	....	87
BONUS SECTION	....	88
REVIEW SECTION	....	89
ALSO BY SHARRON HALSTEAD	....	91

CHAPTER 1

Petite woman
what is petite?

Petite is a size determined by nothing more than height

The definition of

adjective:
petite (of a woman) attractively small and dainty.
"she was petite and vivacious"

synonyms:
small, dainty, diminutive, slight, little, tiny, elfin, delicate, small-boned;

CHAPTER 2
How to dress to suit your *age*

There are so many advantages to being a petite woman, such as:

- You can alter your height as and when you like, enjoying the option of being shorter or taller with the help of heels.

- You can enjoy getting yourself a bargain when shopping in the sales, because you're not the "standard" height.

- You will always look very feminine.

- You suit almost any item of clothing (provided that it's the right fit and style).

- And, you can enjoy looking younger for longer.

The latter doubles up as one of the pros and cons of being slightly shorter in height. Whilst it is great to remain looking youthful for longer, there are of course cases when you do not want to look like a teenager!

One of the main misconceptions about dressing for your age and dressing to look more sophisticated is that you have to wear heels – this is not always the case. The key to dressing to look older and more sophisticated so that you do not get mistaken for a child is to dress in a simple but more sophisticated way.

So what does this mean?

There are certain styles and patterns that are often considered as "younger/teen" types of prints. You should avoid making these mistakes and wearing any of these items if you want to appear older when you dress. Here is what you should avoid:

- Loud prints
- Bold slogans
- Skinny jeans
- Leggings
- Baggy clothing
- Anything with a hood
- Jeans or leggings tucked into knee length boots
- Bright colours
- Neon colours
- Trainers
- Bomber jackets

Here is a list of items that are perfect if you want to look older and smarter when dressing, or if you simply don't want to be mistaken for a teenager:

- Straight leg or bootleg jeans
- Ankle boots
- A tailored style handbag
- Cardigans with delicate button detail
- Pointed toe shoes
- Rich, more expensive looking colours, such as burgundy, light grey, cream, black and white.
- Trench coats
- Blazers
- Plainer clothing with little to no pattern
- A gold or silver watch
- A cross-body bag (worn as a clutch or on one shoulder)
- Shirts and blouses
- Pencil skirts

Below are three examples of looks that do not require wearing heels but are sophisticated looks that will give you a smarter, more elegant appearance.

What is Style and how to *achieve it?*

CHAPTER 3 | 3

Style is not about being fashionable or dressed to perfection 365 days a year, it is about being stylish, comfortable and confident 365 days a year.

Style is a way in which one wears something and presents themselves. Usually a unique way or at least a way that is most comfortable for that person.

Don't confuse style with fashion! It is the biggest mistake that so many people make and this, along with other factors causes confusion. Fashion is the "this and now", it is trends that are popular now. Style however is different. Style is infinitive. We know that we need to develop and understand our own style before we start to develop a wardrobe that we are happy with, but how do we go about doing so? You must start with the basics and not get wrapped up in current fashion trends, designer brands and fashion magazines showcasing how you should dress.

The reason why so many people go wrong with dressing well is because they try to run before they can walk. They go from wearing their tracksuits and comfies one day to wearing an overly detailed outfit possibly fit for a wedding or other special occasion the next day. The result? It never lasts. They revert back to their old ways and why not?! Because that high maintenance style that they thought was right is simply not for them. You'll know that you have found your true style when it feels comfortable and not hard work. Don't get me wrong – you can still look fabulous and glamorous but you have to do it your own way and that is what's so special about personal style building.

Here's a little secret that few people have yet to realise or care to admit: each emerging fashion trend is not a matter of one-size-fits-all. It would be impossible for anybody who is not a catwalk model to carry off each and every fashion look. Following fashion trends religiously without developing your own personal style where you know what suits you is the same as only ever using a sat nav when driving – you can get to places and maybe the sat nav route is not the best, most convenient or the quickest but without your trusty sat nav you would be lost!

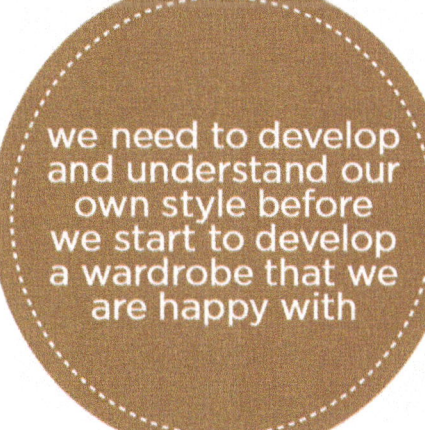

we need to develop and understand our own style before we start to develop a wardrobe that we are happy with

Having your own *personal style* gives you the confidence to accept those off-days and makes you feel comfortable within yourself. Having your own personal style is like having your own brand, you know what it's about, what is not relevant and what would/wouldn't suit it. When you develop your own personal style, you will find shopping so much easier, more enjoyable and far quicker than when you don't know where to start.

As mentioned before, your wardrobe should be made up of 80% clothes and accessories that really suit you and 20% of items that you love too much to care whether they don't suit as well as others. This is the key to a happy wardrobe and creating your own unique style.

Here are some fabulous tips to help you develop and maintain your own super style:

- How tall are you? What is your natural skin tone? What size are you now? Don't think about the skin colour you may have after your two week holiday abroad later in the year, don't think about what will suit you when you are a few lbs lighter or heavier, and don't think about your height when wearing your heels. The way to build great style is being honest with yourself and taking yourself as you are today – pale skin, love handles and all!

- If you love wearing certain clothes but they don't flatter your body shape or skin tone then customise them slightly so that they do suit you, i.e. if you love stripes but you want to avoid horizontal stripes because they make you appear wider, opt for vertical stripes which will elongate and slim out your body.

- If and when you do not feel 100% confident with your weight or appearance, wear stunning accessories and great footwear instead. This will make you feel amazing, confident and glamorous without drawing attention to your so-called problem areas and will stop you from thinking too much about them!

- Avoid high-end and designer clothing when you are just starting to establish your style brand. Designer brands are wonderful but they tend to confuse a lot of people who believe (just like when following fashion trends) that they will be instantly stylish if they stick to designers – which is not true. Another issue with designer clothing and accessories is that you may be so keen to wear them constantly that you never feel stylish or adequate when you are not decked out in brand names.

- Keep it simple! Tackle and master one aspect of your style day by day. Don't copy somebody else's look, especially not a drastic look. Don't rush into buying cloting, footwear or accessories that are overly expensive if you are not completely sure they fit well with your style brand!

Creating your own style and discovering what looks good and suits you may sound like a mammoth task, so you need to take it one step at a time:

1. Start by mastering your perfect look. What do you wear most often? If it's jeans a t-shirt then work on finding the best type of jeans for you (and in the right shades and colours) and look out for the best tops, shirts and jackets that look best too. Perfecting your most worn and most favourite look first will make you feel more confident instantly and will give you the motivation to master other looks too.

2. Go through each look that you would typically wear or would like to wear and experiment with each to find a way of wearing each look to suit your body shape, height, skin tone and of course, your own style tastes! As mentioned above, start with your most favourite and most worn style first before moving on to others. Move through perfecting your best/ideal casual wear look, your best look for the gym, your best formal look, your best summer look, the best coat, the best way to wear bright colours, the best way to wear black, the best way to wear nudes.

3. Remember, a few well fitting garments that you are actually going to wear is much better than a wardrobe full of clothes that you are never going to wear!

TOP TIP: open your wardrobe and ask yourself: how does it make you feel? Do you love the majority of clothes in your wardrobe? Do you love them but don't know how to put them together? Learning these all important style basics, such as how to dress for your body shape, height and skin tone will provide you with the knowledge needed in order not to make mistakes when shopping for clothes or when putting outfits together.

TOP TIP: If the idea of changing the way you transform your clothing into outfits scares you then it is a good idea to spare a little time each week to plan your outfits for the following week. Put aside just 20 minutes each Sunday for example, to put together complete outfits which you can then fold up or hang up in your wardrobe so that you can simply pull them out again as and when you need them, thereby making your morning routine much quicker and far less stressful!

CHAPTER 4

What Not to Wear...

In some cases, some outfits and styles can be worn by one person well but may not suit another person at all, in which case we would say that the second person should not wear that item or look. For e.g. a tall lady of 5 ft 9 could get away with wearing shoes with a thick ankle strap, whereas a lady of 5 ft 1 should avoid shoes with thick ankle straps because they would significantly "shorten" her legs. On the other hand, there are certain dressing and style rules that apply to everyone because there are a definite "no, no!"

Underwear...

- Be mindful of what you plan to wear when choosing your bra. Under no circumstances does a black bra or a coloured bra look good under a pale shirt. When choosing underwear, it is safest to stick to these three co ours: nude/skin colour, black and white.

- Do you wear bras that are too big for you? You must ensure that you wear the right bra and cup size because under a fitted top, it will be visible if your cup size is too big because the bra cup will be very clear to see.

- Do you wear bras that are too tight or too small? The issue with this is that you will get back "overspill" which means your skin and/or curves will hand over the straps of your bra. This is very visible through t-shirts also and just like in any case when you are "spilling out" of your clothing, it is very unflattering too!

- Make sure that your chosen underwear does not exceed the rise of your trousers/bottoms. Your trousers/skirt should not be lower than the rise of your underwear.

Etiquette

- In some cases such as in your working environment, you may not be allowed to wear low cut tops which expose too much of your cleavage or your skin in general.

  In this case you will need to either wear something else or cover up your cleavage and bare skin.

  You can do this by wearing a crop top under your shirt, wearing a vest top underneath, or using a brooch to pin the shirt together at a slightly higher point so that it's not as low cut or revealing.

Sizing Mistakes

> "Your clothes should be tight enough to show you're a woman but loose enough to show you're a lady" – Marilyn Monroe.

- "Your clothes should be tight enough to show you're a woman but loose enough to show you're a lady" - Marilyn Monroe. This is one of the most correct statements about style and fit. It doesn't manner how slim or toned you are, extremely tight fitting clothing is not flattering. Extremely tight clothing doesn't look very good on anybody. Your clothing should "skim" your body rather than showing every bump, muscle, roll and wrinkle!

- To elaborate on the above point, you should not try to squeeze yourself into a size that looks too small on you! Even if you have worn size X all of your life and then go into a store and find that size X is too small and you may need a size or two bigger, do not try to squeeze into your usual size X just because that is the size you wear normally. It doesn't matter how small the size is that you're wearing, if it looks bad and too tight then it's not going to look good at all. Wear the size that looks the best on you, even if that is a size or two bigger than you normally wear. Remember – others around you don't see the size on your labels, they only see how you look in that particular garment/outfit!

- One of the most unflattering ways of dressing is wearing clothing that does not fit properly, no matter whether it is too tight or too big. If you want to go for a look that involves wearing oversized clothing then choose clothing that is in your size but has been made to look oversized is the best idea. Unless you are tall and can carry off wearing clothing that's a couple of sizes too big, as a petite woman you can still carry off the look but it is best to stick to oversized versions of sizes that suit your petite frame. Look for "oversized" or "boyfriend" styles stated on clothing labels in stores.

- On the other hand, wearing clothing that is too small and that you "spill out of" is perhaps worse than wearing clothing that is too big. If you struggle to move in your clothing or have to go to great lengths to make them look as though they fit and are not too tight then you probably need a size bigger. Having to leave a button undone or having to spend more than 2 minutes getting a pair of trousers on is a telltale sign that they are perhaps too tight!

- Both of the above style errors devalue the look of an outfit, making it appear far less expensive than what it actually cost. Clothing that is too big or small resembles that of hand-me-downs, something that younger siblings have to experience. Among children it is cute to see them wearing their older sibling's former clothing but in adults it's not a good look. Even if you are on a budget when shopping, it is still possible to find clothing that fits well by observing your natural body shape and sticking only to ga ments and fits that suit your shape!

Top tip for determining whether your clothing is too tight: after you have worn your clothing for a few hours, observe how your body looks afterwards. Are there any marks? Is your skin a different colour in parts (not due to a sun tan but caused by poor fitting clothing)? Not only is wearing extremely tight clothing a bad look in terms of style, you can also risk damaging your health by doing so, as it can restrict blood flow and circulation.

CHAPTER 5

A Look-book of Ideal Clothing And Accessories for

Petite Ladies

Handbags

Scarves

Sun Glasses

Sun Glasses

Scarves

Evening Wear

Evening Wear

36

Swimsuits

Bras

CHAPTER 6

Different Body *Shapes*

Apple | Pear | Hourglass And Banana/Straight

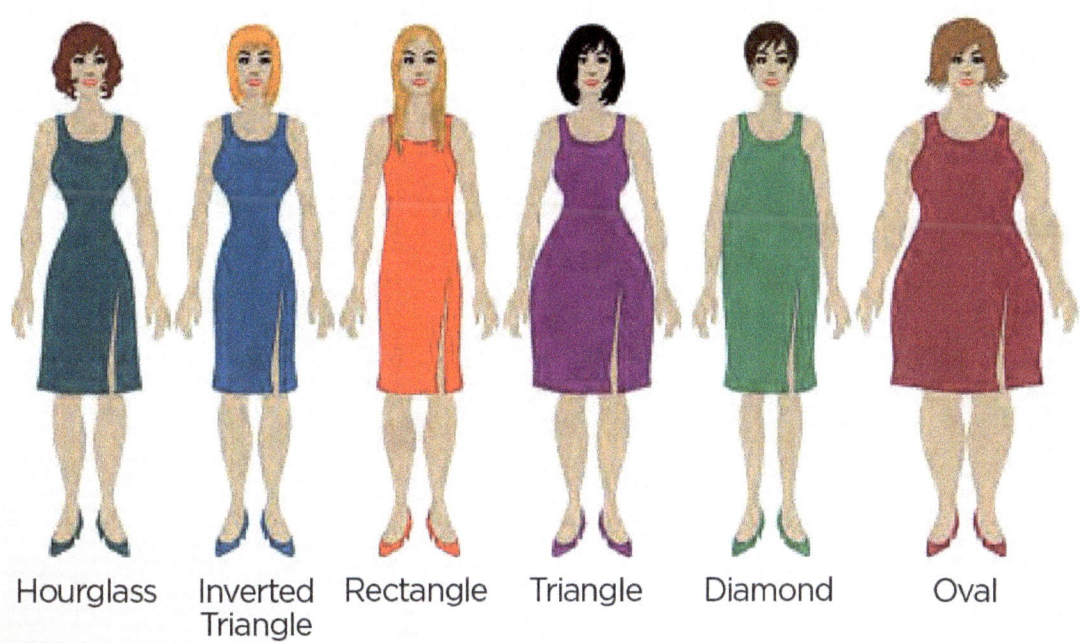

Hourglass | Inverted Triangle | Rectangle | Triangle | Diamond | Oval

Apple shapes

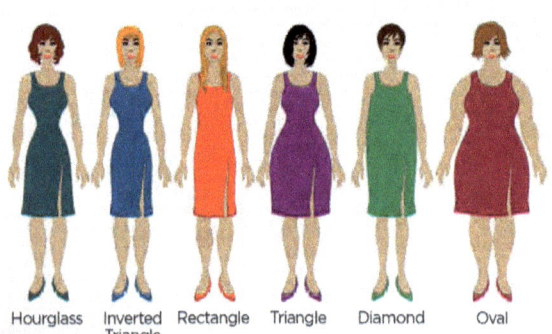

What is an Apple Shape?

An apple body shape, as you can see above, is a body shape where the tops of your arms, your bust, waist and sometimes face are rounder or wider than the bottom half of your body. Typically, those with an apple body shape have noticeably thinner legs and a wider upper body. An apple shape body resembles the shape of an inverted triangle – see below.

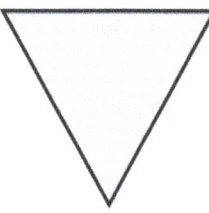

The widest point of an apple body shape is around the shoulder or bust area and gradually narrows towards the hips, which are quite often very narrow in comparison. The name "apple shape" represents the rounder appearance of the upper body.

An Apple Body Shape Means:

- Your widest parts of your upper arms, bust, shoulders, waist and possibly, your face or chin area.

- Your hips are very narrow.

- You have slim, lean legs.

- You rarely gain weight on your hips or below.

- You are least one dress size smaller on your bottom half than you are on your top half.

Adding Height through Clothing

- As somebody with an apple body shape, you will most likely want to add length to your torso. Long, straight fitting tops and jackets are the way to go.

Slimming Down a Petite Frame Using Clothing

- When choosing jackets, you should never go for anything that sits above your hipbone, and especially not at your waistline.

- Blazers are an excellent option for apple body shapes, provided that you choose styles that sit just above, on or slightly below your hipbone. Also, long lapels on the front of the jacket are a must for slimming down a fuller bust and/or stomach area.

- Many ladies who are apple shapes have fuller upper arms too, in which case you need to avoid strappy tops and tube tops/boob tubes and stick to slim fitting short sleeves and slim fitting long sleeves in the summer. Any detail on the sleeve, such as turn ups will make your arms appear fuller, which is why it is best to stick to simple styles.

Elongating Legs & Torso

- Apple shapes usually find that they have shorter bodies, a high hip bone and longer legs. Some ladies who fall into this category of body shape can have an inside leg measurement of 28/29 inches, but the length of their upper body is far shorter. Shorter upper bodies can be difficult to dress because adding even the slightest bit of too much detail can overpower such a small space.

- Skinny trousers and straight leg trousers will elongate your legs. Skinny jeans work better if your upper body is not more than 2 dress sizes larger than your bottom half. Skinny jeans can emphasise the contrast in size and shape between the two halves of your body, which is why slim fitting straight leg jeans that do not grip your ankles at the bottom are the wiser choice.

- When it comes to picking tops, pick loose material that is not too stiff. Fluffy materials or thick woollen jumpers are not a good choice either, as these will make the top half of your body appear fuller. Instead, master the art of layering your clothes gradually.

- A peplum hem on a top will give the illusion of wider hips which will also make your upper body and waist area appear narrower, and is an easy way to fake an hourglass figure.

- In dresses, sleeveless varieties can sometimes work well, provided that the dress comes to your knee.

- When elongating your legs, ensure that cropped jeans and leggings come to above your knee, at your knee or sit at your ankle. Trousers that come to your midcalf are not flattering on even the leanest of legs!

- When trying to elongate either your legs or your torso, try to stick to simple colours and avoid patterns or too much detail on garments.

Understanding Patterns and Prints

- On your upper body avoid fluffy materials, fine detail, small floral patterns, and horizontal stripes.

- On your upper body opt for very little detail, soft and flexible fabrics, and horizontal stripes - also avoid shirts and blouses that are not long and a looser straight fit.

- On the lower half of your body you can wear horizontal stripes, patterns, bold prints, bright colours and a variety of materials. Bottoms with a lot of detail, such as combat trousers with pockets, buttons and patterns will help to balance out your body shape.

- Smaller patterns and prints are more likely to make you look fuller than larger patterns and prints will however, both are best to be avoided on "problem areas."

Ideal Looks for Apple Shape – Day, Night and Skirts and Dresses

Pear shapes

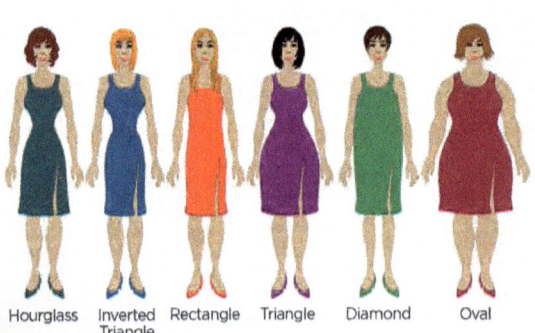

What is Pear Shape?

Pear shape body shapes (as seen above) are bottom-heavy body shapes. They are referred to as "pear shape" because they majority of the weight and width is held at the bottom half of the body, primarily towards the hips, butt and thigh area. Generally, pair shape body shapes have a slim, narrow and leaner upper body and a fuller lower body.

Pear Shape Means:

- Your lower body may be at least one dress size bigger than your upper body
- You are prone to carrying most weight on your hips, thighs and butt.
- You have a narrower upper body and rarely gain weight on your upper body.
- Your waist size is 5 or more inches smaller than your hip measurement.

Adding Height through Clothing

The main area that you need to focus on if you have a pear shape body shape is the lower half of your body because this is the part that may look the widest and shortest. To elongate your legs, you must:

- Wear trousers that do not have a thick waist band.

- Avoid bottoms made from thick material.

- Avoid trousers such as cords, combats and wide leg trousers.

- Wide leg trousers will make your lower body appear as wide as the width of the trousers, which is why they are best avoided. Instead choose straight leg trousers that skim your legs rather than cling to them. Also, avoid attention grabbing materials, such as lycra, leather, velvet, suede etc.

- Choose bottoms with a higher waist line. A decent pair of high waist trousers would be a good idea.

- When choosing skirts, an A-line skirt would work better than a pencil skirt.

- For cropped leggings and trousers, choose either knee length varieties or ankle length varieties. Avoid cropped leggings that come to your mid-calf because these will make your calves look far wider than they really are and this style is unflattering on all body shapes and sizes.

Slimming Down a Petite Frame Using Clothing

- Avoid patterned trousers, stick to plainer colours and styles

- Avoid lots of detail on bottoms – i.e. lots of buttons, pockets, zips, etc.

- Keep your bottoms plain and opt for more interesting patterns on top to balance out the difference between your upper and lower body.

- When choosing jeans opt for darker colours or choose a size up or a looser fitting style in lighter jeans such as stonewash and white.

- When choosing jeans, try to find a pair that are dark on the outside of the leg and lighter in the middle. This is like "contouring for legs" – it will shrink the width of your bottom and legs.

- Be mindful when choosing back pockets on trousers.

- If you want to slim down your derrière then opt for larger back pockets and these will make this area look smaller. On the other hand, if you are trying to fake a larger bottom then go for smaller back pockets.

- Avoid thick materials or boxy materials. Choose softer, more moveable fabrics to help prevent further contrast in your body shape.

Elongating Legs & Torso

- When elongating your legs, ensure that cropped jeans and leggings come to above your knee, at your knee or sit at your ankle. Trousers that come to your midcalf are not flattering on even the leanest of legs!

- When trying to elongate either your legs or your torso, try to stick to simple colours and avoid patterns or too much detail on garments.

- Longer tops that sit slightly below your hipbone will give you a longer looking and slimmer torso. Items such as sleeveless shirts work great for doing this.

Understanding Patterns and Prints

- Smaller patterns and prints are more likely to make you look fuller than larger patterns and prints however, both are best to be avoided on "problem areas."

- Avoid lots of detail on garments worn on your lower body, as this will make your bottom half appear wider and could make your entire body seem out of proportion.

- The buttons and detail on the outer sides of most combat trousers draw attention to these areas and make your lower body appear fuller.

Ideal Looks for Pear Shape – Day, Night and Skirts and Dresses

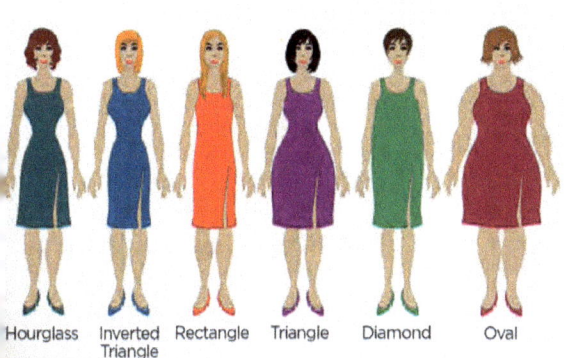

What is an Hourglass Shape?

As you will see from the diagram above, an hourglass figure is a body shape that is equal like the banana body shape but with a noticeably smaller waist and a fuller bust and hips. The one main problem that many hourglass shape ladies have is that they need to dress to accentuate their tiny waists if they want to avoid looking as full as their fullest areas (i.e. their bust and butts) all over their bodies.

Pear Shape Means:

- Your waist is at least 10 inches smaller than your bust and hip measurements
- Your bust and hip measurements are almost equal
- You gain the most weight on your bust, hips, thighs and butt
- You have very small wrists and ankles.
- Your figure appears very balanced.

Adding Height through Clothing

- Adding a waist belt to highlight where your waist is will elongate your torso and legs.

- Trouser suits, jump suits and high waisted trousers work well in adding height to your particular type of body shape.

Slimming Down a Petite Frame Using Clothing

- Don't be afraid to dress for your shape and show off your tiny waist and ample curves!

- Due to having a fuller bust, you must accentuate where your bust starts and ends – a good bra is essential. You must also accentuate your waistline in order not to 'shorten' your upper body.

- Wrap tops and dresses will slim down your figure. Remember to wear fitted clothes rather than baggy clothes which can make your figure appear fuller.

- V-neck tops will highlight your hourglass figure in an enviable yet elegant way.

- Avoid round neck tops which will make your proportions appear unbalanced.

Elongating Legs & Torso

- When trying to elongate either your legs or your torso, try to stick to simple colours and avoid patterns or too much detail on garments.

- Wearing high waisted trousers will elongate your legs and emphasise your enviable waist.

- Avoid detail around the hip area, instead (if wearing clothing with detail) make sure that the detail is around the waist area or along the neckline.

- Blazers with long lapels work well in elongating and slimming down your torso, just be sure to find a tailored blazer with long lapels and that sits at least at your hipbone.

Understanding Patterns and Prints

- Smaller patterns and prints are more likely to make you look fuller than larger patterns and prints however, both are best to be avoided on "problem areas."

- Polka dots, gingham and other traditional patterns look wonderful on hourglass figures.

- Avoid loud prints and slogans, which will make your figure appear fuller without putting any emphasis on your enviable shape.

- Don't be afraid to dress for your shape and show off your tiny waist and ample curves!

Ideal Looks for Hourglass Shape

Straight shapes

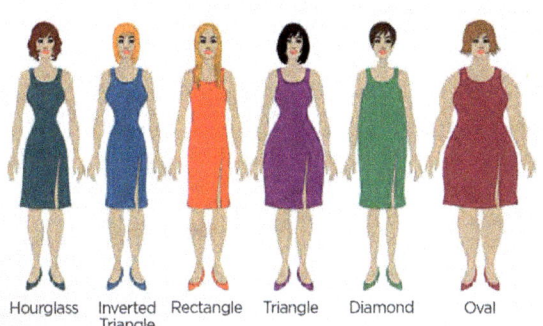

What is a Straight Body Shape?

There are many names for straight body shapes, including: banana (as shown above), ruler, lean tower, balanced, athletic, celery, and many more. Some of these descriptive words can seem a little intimidating and they can also be a little misleading too. So as to be very clear on what a "straight figure" actually is, we are going to refer to this type of body shape as a straight body shape rather than using any of the above mentioned names.

Now, although most people with straight figures are usually very slim, having a straight figure doesn't necessarily mean that you are going to have the long, lean figure of a catwalk model. Many athletes, despite being slightly curvaceous because of their muscle, may also have straight body shapes.

A straight body shape means:

- Your shoulders, waist and hips are all about the same width (with less than 5 inches between them all).

- You do not have any dominant body feature.

- You have slim, equal limbs.

- Generally, your figure is very equal and balanced with no obvious part that is noticeably larger or wider.

- You normally wear the same dress size on both the top and bottom half of your body.

Adding Height through Clothing

- Usually, you will find that either your legs or your upper body are longer – normally you will find that one area usually appears longer. You can add height to your frame by choosing to accentuate your longer half of your body by wearing an item of clothing that will accentuate the longer half of your body. If it's your legs, then wear a great pair of jeans to show off your long legs, if it's your upper body then wear a tailored fitting short to show off your long, lean torso.

- Stick to straight styles rather than flared styles of garments. Long straight coats, long straight leg trousers and jeans, and straight slim fitting tops will make you appear taller, whereas flared garments, bomber jackets and A-line styles will make you appear shorter.

Slimming Down a Petite Frame Using Clothing

- If you have a straight figure then chances are that you will gain a little weight all over rather than in one particular area. To slim your figure down you must not focus on one particular area because this can make your body appear out of proportion. Instead choose slim fitting clothing for your upper and lower body. Straight leg jeans that are darker on the outside and lighter in the middle, tops that reach your hip bone and jackets that end slightly below your hips are all a good example of slimming clothing for straight figured petite ladies!

Elongating Legs & Torso

- The good thing about having an equal/straight body shape is that you can get away with wearing items that other body shapes may not suit. Skinny jeans, shirts, sleeveless shirts are all items that would look great on you and help to elongate certain areas of your body.

- Longer tops that sit slightly below your hipbone will give you a longer looking and slimmer torso. Items such as sleeveless shirts work great for doing this.

- High waisted jeans also look fantastic on balanced, straight figures, as you won't have a muffin top to hang over the waist band of the jeans, making them more flattering. High waisted straight or skinny jeans and trousers will make your legs appear longer and leaner.

- When trying to elongate either your legs or your torso, try to stick to simple colours and avoid patterns or too much detail on garments.

- A peplum hem on a top will give the illusion of wider hips which will also make your upper body and waist area appear narrower, and is an easy way to fake an hourglass figure.

- Choose vertical stripes in clothing for your upper and lower body, as vertical stripes elongate limbs and areas of your body – whereas horizontal stripes do the opposite.

Understanding Patterns and Prints

- When you have a straight figure, any pattern and print will suit you. Athletic, balanced and straight figures can even risk mixing bold patterns and prints on both their upper and lower body.

- Fluffy fabrics and woollen garments are excellent materials to wear on your upper body to create the illusion of a fuller looking bust.

- If you want to create fuller looking hips and thighs, patterned leggings, coloured jeans and pencil skirts are the perfect option!

Ideal Looks for Straight Shape

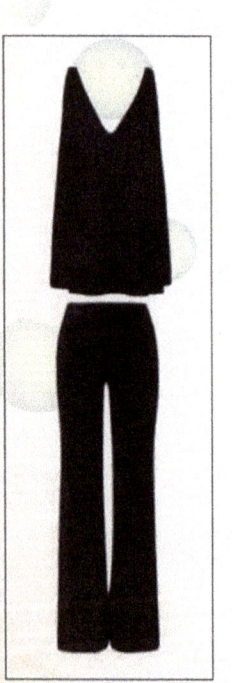

When you have a straight figure, any pattern and print will suit you. Athletic, balanced and straight figures can even risk mixing bold patterns and prints on both their upper and lower body.

High waisted jeans also look fantastic on balanced, straight figures, as you won't have a muffin top to hang over the waist band of the jeans, making them more flattering. High waisted straight or skinny jeans and trousers will make your legs appear longer and leaner.

CHAPTER 7

Size Guide to *Petite sizes*

International Clothing Size Guide

Petite = 5 ft 3 and under

Euro size	Australia size	UK size	Length (CM)	Circumference (CM)
35	1	2	233.31	234.5
36	2	3	239.98	239.0
37	3	4	246.65	243.5
38	4	5	253.32	248.0

UK Sizes (inches)	XS (6)	S (8-10)	M (12-14)	L (16-18)	XL (20-22)	XXL (24-26)
Bust	33"	34-35"	36-37"	$38^{1/2}$-40"	$41^{1/2}$-$43^{1/2}$"	$45^{1/2}$-$47^{1/2}$"
Waist	25"	26-27"	28-29"	$30^{1/2}$-32"	$33^{1/2}$-$35^{1/2}$"	$37^{1/2}$-$39^{1/2}$"
Hips	35"	36-37"	38-39"	$40^{1/2}$-42"	$43^{1/2}$-$45^{1/2}$"	$47^{1/2}$-$49^{1/2}$"
Arm length (petite)	29"	$29^{1/4}$ - $29^{1/2}$"	$29^{3/4}$ – 30"	$30^{1/4}$-$30^{1/2}$"	$30^{3/4}$-$30^{7/8}$"	$33^{7/8}$-34"

International Bra Sizes & Guide

A common issue among ladies with small bone structure is that they require a small band size in their bra but need a larger cup size. For e.g. you may try a bra that's a UK size 34A but find that the band is too large for the size of your back but the cup fits fine. In this case you need to go down a band size and up a cup size – this is a handy trick to know if you do not have the opportunity to go for a professional bra fitting or in the case that a bra you've tried doesn't fit the same way that others in that size do.

Here below is the full list of "petite bra sizes" and their international size equivalents.

AUSTRALIA / NZ	USA	UK / INDIA	EUROPA / CHINA / JAPAN / HONG KONG / KOREA	FRANCE / SPAIN / BELGIUM
8AA	30AA	30A	65A	80A
8A	30A	30B	65B	80B
8B	30B	30C	65C	80C
8C	30C	30D	65D	80D
8D	30D	30DD	65E	80E
8DD	30DD	30E	65F	80F
10AA	32AA	32A	70A	85A
10A	32A	32B	70B	85B
10B	32B	32C	70C	85C
10C	32C	32D	70D	85D
10D	32D	32DD	70E	85E
10DD	32DD	32E	70F	85F

AUSTRALIA / NZ	USA	UK / INDIA	EUROPA / CHINA / JAPAN / HONG KONG / KOREA	FRANCE / SPAIN BELGIUM	AUSTRALIA / NZ	USA	UK / INDIA	EUROPA / CHINA / JAPAN / HONG KONG / KOREA	FRANCE / SPAIN BELGIUM
10E	32DDD/F	32F	70G	85G	14F	36F	36G	80H	95H
10F	32F	32G	70H	85H	14G	36G	36H	80I	95I
10G	32G	32H	70I	85I					
12AA	34AA	34A	75A	90A					
12A	34A	34B	75B	90B					
12B	34B	34C	75C	90C					
12C	34C	34D	75D	90D					
12D	34D	34DD	75E	90E					
12DD	34DD	34E	75F	90F					
12E	34DDD/E	34F	75G	90G					
12F	34F	34G	75H	90H					
12G	34G	34H	75I	90I					
14A	36A	36B	80B	95B					

Shoe Size Conversion Chart

A combination of Foot Length, Width and Arch comprises a person's exact shoe size. Example if 2 people have the same foot length but their width and arch is different they WILL wear different size shoes.

Australia	US	Europe	UK	Asia	China	Foot Length (cm)	Foot Width (Girth) cm	Foot Arch (cm)
1	2	32	13	210	32	18-20	20	21
2	3	33	1	215	33	19-20	21	21
2.5	4	34	1.5	220	34	19-20	22	23
3	4.5	34.5	2	225	34.5	21.5		
3.5	5	35	2.5	230	35	22.8		
4	5.5	36	3	235	36	23.1		
4.5	6	37	3.5	240	37	23.5		

How to find your size

- **Foot Girth**
  - Measure in bare foot
  - Measure the widest part of each foot
- **Foot Length**
  - Measure in bare foot
  - Straight-line from bottom line to top
- **Foot Arch**
  - Measure in Barefoot
  - Measure around the arch of the foot

Components of Petite Peds Shoes

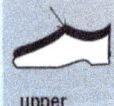 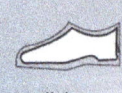 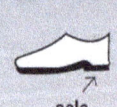   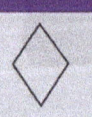

upper   lining   sole   leather   coatd   textile   other material

www.petitepeds.com

Biography

Sharron Halstead is the Founder of Petitepeds, a global online shoe store catering exclusively to ladies with petite feet.

After receiving a multitude of enquiries, comments, complaints, expletives from customers who were fed-up of being treated like second class citizens by the fashion houses, Sharron and her team went about writing "Petite Fashion – The Long and Short of It" to help petite ladies find their own style and sass, and not be at the mercy of a fashion retail world catering primarily to the average size body and foot, but rather use their unique advantage to get the best out of it.

From humble beginnings out of her garage in Melbourne, Australia, she has spread her wings into global markets to assist all petite ladies, the world over, find themselves, their confidence and their self esteem by learning about the basics on how to dress their unique body shapes and petite feet.

Dear Petite Lady,

As a thank you for purchasing this book, I'd like to give you a **FREE E-Book** specifically written to help you on your journey in transforming your Personal Style and Image.

Please visit

http://bit.ly/petitepeds

to claim your FREE Copy TODAY!

Dear Petite Lady,

hope you enjoyed reading this book as much as I enjoyed putting it together for you. As you can see it is not a book that you read once, but more of a reference library for all things Style for the Petite Lady.

If you enjoyed the book and found it useful, I'd be very grateful if you would post an honest review on our Amazon Page as well as on our Google and Facebook Page.

Your support really does matter and will make a difference, not only to us but also to the countless Petite ladies who want to purchase the book.

I do read all the reviews so I can get your feedback in real time.

Here are the links to leave reviews:

Facebook Review	http://bit.ly/PetitepedsFB
Google Review	http://bit.ly/PetitepedsGoogle
Amazon Review	http://bit.ly/PetiteFashion3

Thank you for your Support!

Yours fashionably

Sharron
Founder, PetitePeds

www.ingramcontent.com/pod-product-compliance
Lightning Source LLC
Chambersburg PA
CBHW061757290426
44109CB00030B/2887